Seasonal Living

Seasonal Living

Living in harmony with nature and the seasons

Antonia Beattie

LANSDOWNE

Contents

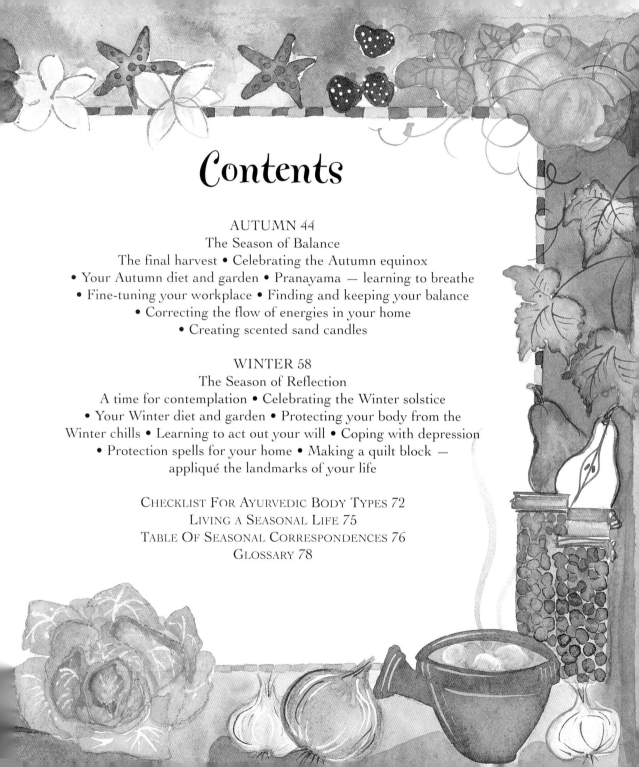

Contents

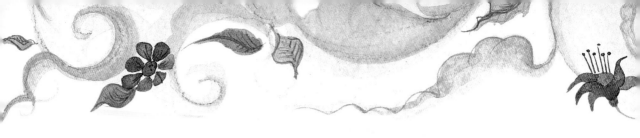

Introduction

"Let sacred knowledge flow to us from all directions"
("Ano bhadrah kratavo yant vishwatah", Rg Veda)

More than ever before we have come to realize that we ignore Nature and her wisdom at our peril. We have reached such a point of technological advance that we now seek something different to help fulfill our lives. There are many people who have found what they seek within the balance generated by observing the natural rhythms and cycles of the world around us. However, technology has allowed the rest of us to ignore these rhythms by giving us such things as air-conditioned rooms and greenhouse-grown fruit and vegetables. But the natural rhythms still flow beneath our artificial environment; so when we feel our lives and endeavors are meaningless and that we are on a perpetual treadmill, perhaps this is because we are separated from nature.

The rhythm of the seasons were viewed by the ancient civilizations, such as the Chinese, as important phases not only for the earth but for human beings as well. The cycles of our life follow the same basic pattern as the cycles of a seasonal year. Those with gardens know that Spring is one of the best times for planting seedlings, while Summer is the time when the plants are allowed to grow, and Autumn is the time to reap the harvest. Winter is the quiet time when most plants are slumbering, gathering their energies for a fine burst of energy again in Spring.

Unfortunately, modern civilization does not allow us a similar cycle through our everyday lives. We are constantly on the move. We have deadlines and commitments that tire us and often leave us with a sense of futility and a longing for something deeper and much more fundamental. Attuning to the cycle of the seasons can help fill that gap.

In Celtic mythology the cycle of the four seasons is called the "Wheel of the Year". A story is told of the love between the archetypal earth god and goddess which led to an enduring seasonal cycle of birth, growth, maturation, decline and death of the earth. It is interesting that in Chinese traditions, the cycle of the seasons is also seen in terms of the rise and fall of male (yang) and female (yin) energy.

This book seeks to find the balance between living comfortably away from nature's harsh extremes and maintaining a powerful connection with the ebb and flow of the earth's cycles. Air conditioning, electricity, hot and cold running water need not get in the way of understanding these cycles as long as we are mindful of keeping these conveniences from harming the earth's environment. This book incorporates the wisdom and knowledge of the West and the long-lived civilizations of China and India, which not only achieved technological advancement but also taught the prudence of understanding the laws and rhythms of Nature.

It is this knowledge that must be celebrated and understood if we are to achieve all the things we really want from life in terms of lifestyle and health. On many levels the stability of the cycles and the regularity of their rhythms can be a soothing one, especially as we see that the wisdom of the ancients is as valid today as it was thousands of years ago.

Ancient Wisdom
Learn the will of nature.
Study it, pay attention to it,
and then make it your own.
Epictetus 15 AD - 135 AD

Seasons of Change
Your body and the seasons

The idea that human beings can fall roughly between three or four body types is one that gained popularity in the West in the late twentieth century. Four body types evolved that were linked to primary glands in the body.

The four body types are:
- **adrenal type** with his or her stocky, muscular build;
- **gonad type** with her (female only) wide hips and small breasts;
- **pituitary type** with his or her plump body and small hands and feet; and
- **thyroid type** with his or her slim body and heavy thighs.

Each type has a particular taste preference, weight distribution and hormonal balance. The concept of body types in ancient systems has often been linked to seasonal times and the corresponding elements. In Chinese medicine, there are five seasons which correspond with the following five elements, predominant organs and numbers.

Table of Chinese seasons and correspondences

SEASON	ELEMENT	ORGANS	NUMBERS
Spring	*Wood*	*Liver* *Gallbladder*	*3, 4*
Summer	*Fire*	*Heart* *Small intestine*	*9*
Late summer	*Earth*	*Stomach, Spleen* *Pancreas*	*2, 5, 8*
Autumn	*Metal*	*Lungs, Large Intestine*	*6, 7*
Winter	*Water*	*Bladder, Kidney*	*1*

In Ayurvedic medicine, there are only three body types or *prakruti*, called kapha, pitta and vata. However, a person can also be a combination of any two prakruti. As in Chinese medicine, which is said to have been derived from the ancient Indian Ayurvedic system, these prakruti correspond with the following seasons and elements.

- kapha corresponds with Spring and is a combination of earth and water;
- pitta corresponds with Summer and is a combination of fire and water; and
- vata corresponds with Winter and is a combination of ether and air.

It is believed that each prakruti must take particular care of his or her body during the corresponding season. The characteristics of each prakruti are:

- a kapha type is usually thick set with wide shoulders and hips and has a tendency to store energy and fat;
- a pitta type is generally of medium height, size and weight and experiences an even flow of energy; and
- a vata type is naturally slim with narrow shoulders and hips and experiences an erratic flow of energy.

See pages 72, 73 and 74 for a checklist to determine your Ayurvedic body type.

kapha   *pitta*   *vata*

Seasonal energies and colors

In many of the ancient systems, there is a belief that the world is made up of a number of elements. In traditional Chinese thinking, each season is linked with a form of energy, a concept echoed in many of the other ancient traditions. The Chinese believe that the world is made up of five elements — fire, earth, metal, water and wood.

The season of Spring is linked with the element of wood. The energy of wood and the season is one of rising energy, of growth. It is a yang energy, highly unpredictable and unstable but filled with enthusiasm and a feeling of great potential. Colors that correspond to this season include those that relate to the color of young saplings, such as light greens, and a sky that is emerging from its Winter grays, such as light blues.

The season of Summer is linked with the element of fire. The energy is yang in this season. There is a sense of ripening and blossoming, that the trees will be bearing fruit and the ground will yield many of the vegetables planted in the Spring. The energy has matured and intensified, creating a strong, sustained vitality. Colors that correspond with this season include bright blues, reds and oranges.

The season of Late Summer in the Chinese system, which is the shortest season of the year, is linked with the element of earth. In the Northern Hemisphere, the season occurs between 31 July and the Autumn Equinox in mid September. In the Southern Hemisphere, it occurs between 31 January until the Autumn equinox in mid March. It is also the balance between the yang and yin energies, the male and female energies respectively. The energy is the balance between the first harvest and the last fruiting. Colors that correspond with this season include yellows, light orange and golden hues.

The season of Autumn is linked with the element of metal. The energy now is predominantly yin as it seeks to expend its final goodness. This is the time of the gathering in of the energy so that it can be stored for Winter. Colors that correspond with this season include white and other pale colors, symbolizing the waning of the intensity of color, leaving behind the pale husks.

The season of Winter is linked with the element of water. The energy is almost entirely yin and there is a sense of the energy being conserved. Winter's energy has gone underground but there is still growth going on beneath the earth's surface. Colors that correspond with this season include black, browns and other dark colors.

The arrows around the circle show the flow of energy between the Elements representing the seasons.

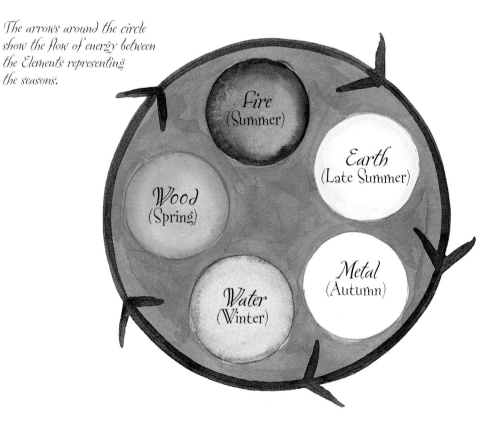

Seasonal eating

Eat to live not live to eat — Proverb

One of the best ways of adapting to seasonal living is by linking into what the earth is producing during the various seasons. The Chinese were well aware of how influential the seasons were on their health. With each season, the Chinese would eat different foods prepared in different ways. For example, in Summer, light vegetables with a high moisture content would be eaten, cooked quickly in the wok. During Winter, root vegetables were eaten more, and longer cooking processes, such as baking, were used. Eating only seasonal foods is also a very cost effective way of buying fruit and vegetables. Vegetables and fruit in season cost considerably less than their greenhouse counterparts in other times of the year. In Chapters 2–5, seasonal food tables are included. These tables are only a guide and are subject to seasonal differences in different areas. Make friends with an organic farmer living near you and customize the tables for your own area.

Spring diet

Your Spring diet must contain more leafy greens than animal foods. The foods that will enable your body to tap into the sense of enthusiasm and creativity must be light, such as salads or quickly stir-fried vegetables, such as squash, beans, broccoli, zucchini and green peppers (capsicum) and other green vegetables with a high water content. Don't forget to include rocket with your salad or in sandwiches. The emphasis in this season is on light, almost vegetarian, meals. Stir fries can be served on a bed of wheat pasta or rice noodles.

Summer diet

Your Summer diet continues with a predominantly vegetarian emphasis. Salads, fresh fruits, clear soups and vegetable stir fries on beds of long-grain rice will help your body cope with the Summer heat. Preparation of food during this season should be quick and without too much fuss. To keep feeling well during Summer, it is important to keep to a minimum heavy animal foods, alcohol and fried foods. However, you can try grilling or quickly steaming fish or even chicken, or investigating other non-animal protein foods, such as soybean products.

Autumn diet

Your Autumn diet allows more protein, either animal foods or soybean products, such as tofu, and various legumes. The emphasis in this season is on orange and yellow vegetables, including sweet potato, carrots and, of course, pumpkin. Food can be cooked for much longer. You may consider warming stews, pies and baked vegetables. Incorporate ginger and garlic in your cooking, as well as cabbage, celery, cauliflower and turnips. Grains are also important to eat in this season, your ideal choice being short-grain rice.

Winter diet

Your Winter diet aims to keep you warm during the cold months of Winter. Continue using ginger and garlic in your cooking as both are good for circulation of the blood. The foods that are stored for Winter always need longer cooking time, such as stewing, steaming, roasting or baking. Root vegetables are in abundance. Baked potatoes and pumpkin pies feature strongly on a Winter menu, as do hearty soups or casseroles made with root vegetables, legumes, short-grain rice and/or meat.

Celebrating the Seasons

In Celtic mythology, eight festivals are celebrated to mark the passage of the seasons through the year. The eight festivals are collectively referred to the "Wheel of the Year", depicted as a wheel with eight spokes. The festivals occur at approximately six-weekly intervals throughout the year. Four of the festivals fall on the equinoxes and solstices, the dates of which vary slightly from year to year. Equinoxes are days when night and day are equal due to the sun crossing the equator. Solstices are times when the sun is as far as possible away from the equator, causing the longest day which heralds Summer and the longest night which is the forerunner to Winter. These festivals, which mark the changes of the four seasons, generally occur according to the table below:

Table of solstices and equinoxes

SOLSTICE/ EQUINOXES	ANOTHER NAME	NORTHERN HEMISPHERE DATE (VARIES)	SOUTHERN HEMISPHERE DATE (VARIES)
Winter Solstice	Yule	21-23 December	21-23 June
Spring Equinox	Ostara	21-23 March	21-23 September
Summer Solstice	Litha	21-23 June	21-23 December
Autumn Equinox	Mabon	21-23 September	21-23 March

The Wheel of the Year echoes an old Celtic myth which marks the birth, life and death of the sun god. In Winter, the goddess gives birth to a baby god who begins his adolescence during the Spring equinox and comes to maturity at Summer solstice. At this time he is at the height of his powers and he plants his seed within the goddess. It is also a bittersweet time as he begins to leave his strength behind, feeling increasingly weaker until he dies, leaving room for his successor, a newborn child. From midsummer, the goddess's power is increasing while her child grows within her during Autumn. On the shortest day of the year, at Winter solstice, a boy child is again born who carries on the tradition of his father for the new year.

By celebrating the festivals with the appropriate foods, symbols and rituals, the ancient Celts kept in rhythm with the seasons, tapping into and understanding the strengths of Mother Earth.

The other four festivals fall on dates that represent the highest energy in the season and are shown in the table below:

Table of the other seasonal festivals

SEASON	ANOTHER NAME	NORTHERN HEMISPHERE DATE	SOUTHERN HEMISPHERE DATE
Autumn	Halloween	31 October	1 May
Winter	Candlemas	2 February	1 August
Spring	May Day	1 May	31 October
Summer	Lammas	1 August	2 February

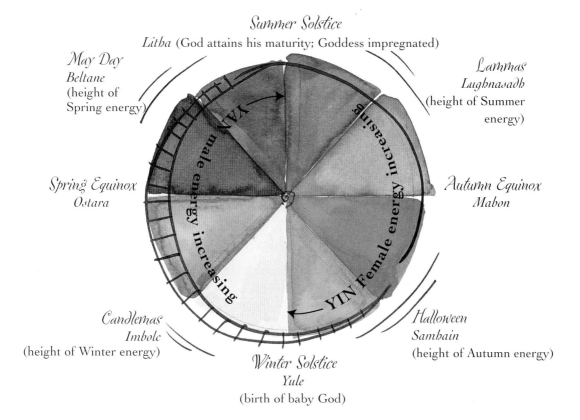

Summer Solstice
Litha (God attains his maturity; Goddess impregnated)

May Day
Beltane
(height of
Spring energy)

Lammas
Lughnasadh
(height of Summer
energy)

YANG male energy increasing

YIN Female energy increasing

Spring Equinox
Ostara

Autumn Equinox
Mabon

Candlemas
Imbolc
(height of Winter energy)

Halloween
Samhain
(height of Autumn energy)

Winter Solstice
Yule
(birth of baby God)

SPRING
The Season of Growth
New beginnings
Now is the time to get serious about living your ideals.
Epictetus (55 AD – 135 AD)

Spring starts with the vernal or Spring equinox in March (Northern Hemisphere) or in September (Southern Hemisphere). The planting of seeds in your garden or window box is echoed in the planting of new ideas and resolutions for your new sacred year. Sometimes, to allow space for the new, the old must be cleansed or cleared away. In this chapter we discuss a number of traditional cleansing therapies for your body (see pages 20 and 21) and prepare a "treasure map" to help you implement changes in your life (pages 24 and 25). Once you have cleansed yourself, you might also feel the urge to cleanse the energies in your home. The principles of feng shui, the Chinese art of design and placement, are outlined on pages 26 and 27. Your career and lifestyle may also require some new energy or even change (see pages 22 and 23).

This is a fairly unstable time, particularly with the shaking up of the old energy and the coming in of the new. Many people feel that about the time of Beltane/May Day — the height of the energies in Spring — major changes can occur. Some of these changes may appear to be destructive, such as the ending of a treasured relationship. Make sure you look at what other opportunities have opened to you. The Spring equinox is the time of equal light and dark in the world, with the light increasing toward Summer. Many of the changes that occur will be constructive, despite how despondent you may feel at the time. A creative project that helps you weave new and beautiful strands of threads and ribbons symbolizing your dreams and ambitions can be found on pages 28 and 29.

Celebrating the Spring equinox

"In the Spring a young man's fancy lightly turns to thoughts of love."
Lord Alfred Tennyson (1809 – 1892) Locksley Hall

The first day of Spring bears a great sense of energy and promise. With the increase of the sun's energy, the emphasis at the Spring equinox is on fertility. Your creativity and the earth's productivity both start to gather momentum. This is the time to free yourself from Winter's slumbers and to feel a sense of your own strength and beauty. Traditional forms of celebrating the Spring or vernal equinox revolve around putting energy back into the earth with rituals involving the planting of flowers, trees and herbs. A blessing that dedicates each planting to the earth may be said or felt as the plant or seed is inserted into the ground.

Approximately six weeks after the Spring equinox is another festival called Beltane (also known as May Day in the Northern Hemisphere). This is the height of the Spring energy. It is a highly creative, flagrantly sexual time which is expressed through the many fertility symbols that characterize this festival, such as bonfires, traditionally lit to ensure fertility to the household and farmyard, and dancing around the maypole.

New unions, friendships and business deals are created during this festival, and as we commit to a new path, disruptions in the old energies around us may result. This is part of the cleansing energy of Spring.

Your Spring diet and garden

The season of Spring is your opportunity to learn a new way of eating, to experiment with different concepts and dietary ideas. Spring can be an unstable time in terms of weather — one day the heat makes you want to eat salads and raw fruit while the next day a hearty beef stew sounds appetizing, since the temperature has dropped and the mist is rolling in. Use this time to experiment with different taste sensations. This is not yet the right time to begin a regimented food regime but may be the time to revise your food disciplines and make a simple list of a few rules that you know, from past experience, are good for you. Above all else, aim for balance and nutrition.

When deciding on the appropriate diet for you, use the following four questions as a guideline. If you can answer "yes" to the following, you are well on your way to a balanced food regime:

1. Are you eating a wide variety of food, including breads, cereals, fruits, legumes and vegetables?

2. Is your diet one that you can live on for life?

3. Does your diet include foods you like?

4. Does your diet allow you to eat out?

Spring fruits and vegetables

Fruit

End of the red apple season
Green apples (all year round)
End of avocado season
Bananas (all year round)
Blueberries
Dates (all year round)
Grapefruit (all year round)
Lemons (all year round)
Mandarins (early Spring)
Mangos (late Spring)
Oranges (mid Spring)
Papaya (pawpaw)
Pineapple
Plums (late Spring)
Strawberries
Watermelon

Vegetables

Asparagus
Red beet (beetroot)
Broccoli (early Spring)
Brussels sprouts (early Spring)
Button squash
Cabbage (mid Spring)
Carrots (all year round)
Cauliflower (early Spring)
Corn (late Spring)
Green beans (early Spring)
Leeks
Parsnips (mid Spring)
Snow peas (early Spring)
Swedes (early Spring)

Your garden tasks for Spring

The beginning of Spring is the time to sow your Summer vegetables, such as beans, capsicums, carrots, celery, cucumber, lettuce, melons, squash and tomatoes. If you live in a cool, temperate climate which is prone to frost, keep your seedlings under protection until the earth becomes warmer. If you are establishing a vegetable garden, you may consider hedging your vegetable patch with parsley. By mid Spring, you can sow some basil, dill, fennel, and plant the sweet potatoes, lavender, mint, rosemary and sage.

A charm to make your herb garden grow

As you are sowing your seeds, use the little verse below as a mantra to be repeated over and over while you visualize your seedlings growing into healthy plants:

Herbs that charm
Herbs that heal
Know no harm
And charge our meal

Cleansing therapies for your body
"Rouse yourself from the daze of unexamined habit."
Epictetus (55 AD – 135 AD)

Spring is traditionally a time of cleansing. Over time, many different detoxification procedures have evolved that can help you get rid of the toxins accumulated in your body over Autumn and Winter. Toxins can amass as the result of undigested foods in the body and of pollution in your environment. Spring is a particularly bad time for people with allergies or sinus problems as pollen levels in many areas are high. If you suffer from respiratory illnesses, which can be the result of a high level of toxicity in your body, detoxification is very appropriate at this time. Even if your immune system is in good working order, cleansing your body will still be of benefit if you live in the inner city or in a high-pollution neighborhood. Such methods of detoxification as fasting, liver cleansing and lymph draining can lead to the removal of minor health problems, better skin condition, effective stabilization of your weight and the alleviation of depression. The down side is that detoxification can be a fairly grueling process. After 24 hours of commencing a detoxification program, a person can start feeling "headachy", as toxins are released through the body, and can feel embarrassed about their odor as the toxins begin to leave the body through the skin. With headaches, often you will find that if you persist with your program your headache and other side effects will go away, leaving you feeling very well in approximately three days time.

One of the oldest methods for detoxification is fasting. This method of cleansing is the quickest, most straightforward way to cleanse your body of harmful toxins. It involves three days of abstaining from food and drinking only water. Some people find that fasting is not such a shock to the system if, two days before they wish to fast, they only eat vegetables and fruit and drink fresh juices. For those who are prone to sugar imbalances, having two days of eating fruit and vegetables can help the body balance itself before it undergoes the cleanse.

If you suffer from a severe sugar imbalance, you may wish to consult your health practitioner before going through a fast. Also, fasting must not be considered a method for weight loss. As soon as you gradually return to normal eating, you will usually regain the weight you lost during the fast. Also, after a day or so, the body begins to take its energy from your muscles as well as your stored fat. However, fasting can be an excellent start to a new eating regime, which in itself should be the cause of your more gradual weight reduction.

Caution

When considering undertaking a detoxification program, first consult with your health practitioner. Don't undertake detoxification if you are pregnant or breast-feeding or suffer from any eating disorders.

How to initiate new career opportunities: what is your calling?

"Within the divine order, we each have our own special calling.
Listen to yours and follow it faithfully."
Epictetus (55 AD – 135 AD)

What is it you want to do with your life? What do you love to do? There is one school of thought that says we all know perfectly well what we want to do but, for those of us who are not doing what we love, our instincts are overlaid with the expectations of a number of important people in our lives, particularly our families. An entertaining exercise to see exactly all the myriad conflicting images which we were given as children is to cut out pictures from various magazines of the type of person our parents wanted us to be. From this exercise you might see how little cohesion there is in these images, which represent what we are supposed to be.

Sometimes, the type of work you have been doing is a clue to what sort of work you really should be pursuing. A useful exercise is to list all your skills, both in the workplace and as hobbies. Take particular note of the subjects you enjoy and of any activity in which you showed some talent. Often we do not follow up our talents because they are not perceived to be "sensible". Look to see what patterns emerge. List where you have worked, the attitudes of your boss and co-workers, the hours you worked and how you felt in that environment.

By examining your work history, see if you can write in detail what your perfect job would be, isolating aspects that you particularly enjoyed. Take into account the following issues:

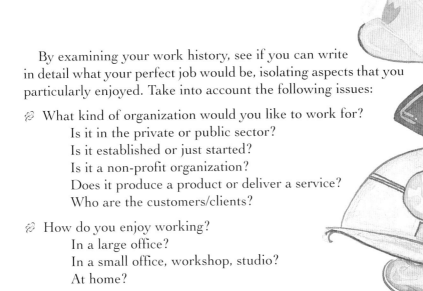

🌿 What kind of organization would you like to work for?
        Is it in the private or public sector?
        Is it established or just started?
        Is it a non-profit organization?
        Does it produce a product or deliver a service?
        Who are the customers/clients?

🌿 How do you enjoy working?
        In a large office?
        In a small office, workshop, studio?
        At home?

🌿 What hours would you prefer to work?
        Regular?
        Flexible?

If you are having trouble visualizing your perfect job, try writing a job description for a job that would make your life totally miserable. This can be even more revealing of what job you really do want. Spring is a good time to assess what you really want to do with your life and to start gathering information about possible career opportunities and further study options.

Planning to change your lifestyle —
making a treasure map

This is a delightful way to hone your visions about how you would like to see your house, life and career. Using pictures taken from magazines, photocopied from books or downloaded from the Internet, the purpose of this exercise is to build up a cache of images that touch a chord within you about what you want from life. Pictures of your ideal home, your wardrobe and where you would like to live can all be stuck onto a large sheet of paper and hung up in a safe space so that you can look at it from time to time. You may also like to include a recent picture of yourself in the center.

After a while, a type of "weeding" process starts to happen — some pictures do not seem quite right. Feel free to continue working on your treasure map, adding and removing images. The more you think in terms of pictures, the more the mind is ready to find opportunities for the images to manifest. These pictures tend to also override any verbal messages we were given as children or young adults that we do not deserve only the best in our lives.

If you do not feel comfortable about pinning up a large sheet, consider purchasing a journal, loose-leaf folder or specially designed folder with clear plastic "pocket" sheets. As you are collecting images, you may become aware that there is a specific area that needs special attention, for example, you want to move house or to change weight. Start a separate journal or folder for your special project, which allows you space to work out your ideas. Once you are satisfied, you should have a strong collection of images that show your visualization in its ideal form.

This is powerful magic. Make sure that you look at your picture or book once a day or at least give it a thought. You may even wish to include a religious symbol of importance to you, such as a cross, ankh or pentacle. You can also include an affirmation focusing on the achievement of the goals of the picture and its harmonious effect on you and everyone else concerned.

Caution

If looking for images to change weight, be careful to find pictures of people who are approximately your body type or bone structure. You may even consider using instead old pictures of yourself when you were at your ideal weight.

Clearing stagnant energies from your house

One of the first things you need to do to clear stagnant energies from your home is to remove all the unwanted material objects that clutter your space. Assess your home, room by room. Do you need to keep all those magazines, books, old saucepans?

Sometimes we keep more material possessions than we need because our direction in life is scattered and unfocused. By fine-tuning what you wish to do with your life (see pages 24 and 25) you will be in a better position to know which objects you don't need anymore. By clearing your living space, you are allowing new energy to come into your home.

Once the junk is out of your life, you will also find that it is easier to keep the house tidy and functional throughout your new year. Decide what activities you most like doing and where in your house you like doing them. Create the space for your activity to happen or make a list of things, such as a table or shelf space, that you need and buy or make these components gradually through the year.

Some old energies can be stubborn and just will not be released by your improving the circulation of energy through your house by removing all unnecessary objects. Many believe that the corners of a room are particularly prone to harboring stagnant energies. Some ways of clearing old energy from a room include clapping your hands or burning incense sticks in each corner.

Another method is to stand in the room you wish to clear and to imagine the energy in the room as a luminous haze. Imagine that your body's energy extends beyond the floorboards into the earth. Feel connected with the earth. This is very important if you contemplate any work with energies around the home, your family or yourself. Move your arms up in a sweeping fashion, imagining that a golden energy from the earth is traveling up your spine and through your arms. Visualize the golden energy looping around the stagnant energy. Draw the energy down to the floor and imagine that the stagnant energy is being drawn back into the earth and that the golden energy is also drawn from you into the ground. Put a bright Spring flower or brightly colored piece of fabric in the room to celebrate the renewal of its energy.

Weaving your hopes and dreams into your life

The idea behind this creative project is to create a weaving that incorporates your ambitions and inspirations for the new sacred year by communicating your intention to the natural world through color and symbols. As the wild winds of Spring cleanse the trees of their dead branches, see if you can find a "V" shape within the crook of two broken branches.

Wherever possible, it is important to use natural fibers to help tap into the earth's energy. You may use cottons, silks, wool and raffia. Within the "V", use twine to create your warp (vertical threads) within which you will be weaving your threads horizontally, creating the weft. There is no need to construct an overall picture. Part of the charm of this project is that it allows your mind to switch into neutral as your body takes over, expressing what it wants from the threads you have collected previously.

Symbols and colors are an important method of linking into and affecting our subconscious mind. The colors specified in the table below correspond with certain attributes. See if these attributes work for you. If not, using the table's list as a guide, devise ones that seem more appropriate to you. If you are so inclined you may wish to experiment with dyeing the threads you have collected, using natural dyes (refer to the table opposite).

Once you have threaded your warp between the branch's arms and have collected and/or dyed your threads and have painted or chosen any ceramic, wooden or metal symbols (maybe in the form of buttons), find a safe and quiet space in your house, garden or favorite retreat. Arrange your work as you feel comfortable, making sure that all the pieces are within easy reach. Before starting, take the time to think about the season and what you want to achieve throughout the new year. From here on, your task is to thread your strands in and out of the warp. As you pick up each thread, affirm in your mind what the thread symbolizes for you.

When you have finished, hang your creation in a spot where you can see it from time to time during the year. It will remind your subconscious of what you are seeking to achieve.

Table of colours, attributes and natural dyes

COLOUR	ATTRIBUTES	NATURAL DYES
Red	Strength	Cochineal
Orange	Creativity	Onion skin
Yellow	Sense of self	Turmeric
Green	Heart	Colts-foot
Blue	Clarity	Blueberries

SUMMER
The Season of Development
Setting yourself free

Summer is a much more stable time than Spring. The vegetables and fruits in the garden are ripening, mirroring the growth of our plans and the flourishing of health in our bodies. We are also gathering herbs from our garden, many of which will help flavor the foods of the season (see page 33).

If we have not nurtured our bodies through Winter and cleansed them in Spring, Summer can be a very hard season to endure. Often the inability to cope with heat is a sign of high levels of toxicity in the body. However, we can combat high toxin levels by taking on such pleasant, cooling exercises as swimming or aqua aerobics that help our lymph glands remove accumulated toxins, as well as helping us to also eliminate stress.

After the tumultuous energy of Spring, Summer is an excellent time to consolidate our energies and make concerted efforts to lose weight (see pages 34 and 35), to take the time to understand what is our calling in life (see pages 36 and 37) and to bring new energies into our home (see pages 40 and 41). This is also a good time to follow a food and exercise regime that is suitable for your body type (see pages 32 and 33) and to practice a series of yogic postures that salute the life-affirming energy of the Sun while integrating your body with your psyche (see pages 38 and 39). Also, learn to make protective amulets this season, the most effective being those that include the herbs that have grown in your garden (see pages 42 and 43).

Celebrating the Summer solstice

The Summer solstice heralds the new season of Summer and represents the time of fulfillment. The Sun is at the highest point in the heavens and the Summer solstice is the longest day of the seasonal year. Decorate your home with sunflowers or other golden-hued flowers to commemorate the occasion for soon the strength of the season will wane; this is echoed during the season as the days become shorter and the light becomes weaker. Summer solstice is also a good time to take stock and attune your life to the Wheel of the Year. Notice the fulfillment of certain of your goals and aims.

Six weeks later, the height of Summer's energy is felt during a festival called Lammas. This festival represents a time of sacrifice where the earth has used the last of its yang energy to bring forth a bountiful harvest of golden fruits, vegetables and grains. It is the celebration of the first of the three major harvests — the grain harvest. Traditionally, the grain harvest is particularly potent because it is linked to the reverence of grain which was associated with the cycles of birth, death and regrowth. It is a time for you to acknowledge the sacrifices that you have made during the year to provide your own harvest, whether it be through monetary gains, love or career advancements. It is a time to understand that how you have worked and what you have sacrificed will be reflected in how bountiful your harvest will be at this time. If your harvest is meager, learn from your mistakes and try again next year.

Your Summer diet and garden

Summer is a time of learning to understand your body's needs. A way of helping you assess your needs is to determine your body type and what that means in terms of your eating habits. In Ayurvedic medicine, there are three types of prakruti or body types (as discussed on page 9). It is believed that each type has its own particular metabolism that reacts favorably to certain foods, and by following simple rules, you will find it easy to shift your weight.

In Summer, people of the pitta type must be particularly vigilant in looking after themselves, as they tend to burn easily in the sun and find the heat difficult to handle. They must also avoid hot foods that are sour, salty or pungent (like garlic). In Ayurvedic medicine, pitta types should concentrate on grains, fruit and vegetables. Bread, caffeine, sugar and tomatoes all tend to react badly with this body type.

Kapha types, who have had their difficulties in Spring because they tend to dislike changes, must avoid sweet, sour and salty foods and concentrate on vegetable-based meals. They do not need to eat too much grain and should avoid overeating legumes and meat.

Vata types should include in their diets a good range of naturally occurring sweet, sour and salty foods. As they may develop allergies to wheat, rice and oats are recommended for vata body types. Raw vegetables and unripe fruits should be avoided while animal products are a must. However, they must not overindulge in too much animal protein. Vata types are also prone to addictions, particularly to nicotine, sugar and caffeine, which further exacerbates their erratic energy levels. Ayurvedic philosophy believes that meditation and relaxation techniques can be more effective in increasing your energy than the use of artificial stimulants.

Summer Fruits and Vegetables

Fruit	Vegetables
Apricots	Asparagus (early Summer)
Blackberries	Butternut pumpkin (late Summer)
Blueberries	Button squash
Cherries	Capsicums (mid Summer)
Figs (late Summer)	Celery (late Summer)
Grapes	Corn
Limes (late Summer)	Tomatoes (mid Summer)
Mangos	
Melons	
Oranges	
Peaches	
Papaya (pawpaw)	
Pears (Williams)	
Plums	
Raspberries	
Cantaloupes (rockmelons)	
Watermelon	

Gardening tasks for Summer

During Summer it is important to keep your plants well watered, fed and mulched. It is also the time to sow vegetables such as beans, red beet (beetroot), cabbage, capsicums, carrots, celery, squash and sweet corn and to pick herbs. It is traditional to pick mistletoe and St. John's wort at Midsummer's Eve. Both these herbs are well known for their magical protective qualities and are traditionally used for making amulets. You might also prepare your garden for Spring bulbs, such as snowdrops, and sow your Winter and Spring flowers, such sweet williams and stocks.

Ancient Wisdom
He who knows others is clever;
He who knows himself has discernment.
He who overcomes others has force;
He who overcomes himself is strong.
Lao-tzu

A Summer routine for losing weight

It cannot be emphasized strongly enough that you must look at yourself very carefully and with a sense of goodwill and nurture before you decide whether you really need to lose weight as opposed to finding an exercise that suits your metabolism. Using the checklist on pages 72 and 73 to determine your Ayurvedic body type or prakruti, follow the simple rules below to help you attain and keep your ideal weight.

For vata types, who tend to carry their extra weight around their midriff, the following suggestions may be useful:

- Foods to include in your diet — sweet, sour or salty foods, such as mangos, lemons and avocados.
- Foods to avoid — bitter, pungent and astringent food, including cranberries, apples and onions. Particularly avoid raw vegetables, wheat, unripe fruit, tobacco, caffeine and sugar.
- Exercise and massage — mild exercise, such as swimming, and a massage, regularly once a month.

For pitta types, whose extra weight tends to distribute itself evenly over their bodies, the following suggestions may be useful:

- Foods to include in your diet — sweet, bitter and astringent, such as grapes, dried fruits and daikon (long white radish).
- Foods to avoid — sour, salty, pungent, including tomatoes, meat, eggs, yeasty bread, alcohol and salt.
- Exercise and massage — team sports and mild exercise such as yoga, and maybe experiment with various forms of energy-balancing massages.

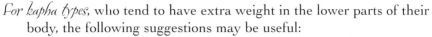

For kapha types, who tend to have extra weight in the lower parts of their body, the following suggestions may be useful:

- Foods to include in your diet — bitter, pungent and astringent foods, such as garlic, lemons and peppers.
- Foods to avoid — sweet, sour and salty foods, such as bananas, dairy products and tomatoes.
- Exercise and massage — vigorous exercise and therapeutic massage to stimulate circulation.

For those who have identified themselves as combined vata/pitta types, follow the vata diet during Autumn and Winter and the pitta diet during Spring and Summer. For pitta/kapha types, follow the pitta diet during late Spring and early Autumn and the kapha diet the rest of the year.

Irrespective of your body type, it is important to keep in mind the following simple rules for weight maintenance:

- *Never eat when you are feeling emotionally unstable or tired.*
- *Never eat immediately after physical exertion.*
- *Fully concentrate on your meal — set aside time to have your meal without distractions.*
- *Only eat when you are feeling truly hungry.*

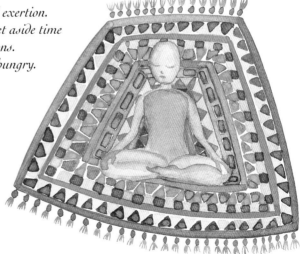

Find your life's work

With enough knowledge and self-confidence, you can do anything.

In Spring you wrote down what your perfect job would be. In Summer you will need to take action to accumulate the necessary information to see if there are any existing jobs or businesses that match your job description or whether you should develop your own business. As Summer is the height of yang energy, this is a good time to talk to people who are already doing your desired work or who are trained to help those wishing to make a career change in their lives. Chats with people already in your chosen area or industry can help you assess what obstacles you might meet in attaining a successful career change and will help you assess whether this path is really for you.

Knowing what obstacles you can come across is invaluable as this gives you time to work out your strategies and your contingencies plan. To make a successful career change, it is important that you feel in control of your new path. It is equally important to give yourself enough time and information so that you are able to steer your way to your goal rather than allowing a string of events trigger reactive behavior, which could possibly damage your chance of success. Do not count on the occasional success story in which someone lands his or her perfect job without really trying. Ask yourself how that person came to be in the right place at the right time.

However, there are ways that you can stack the odds in your favor. According to the Bagua, a grid system sometimes used in feng shui, the career or life-path sector of your home is the section where you enter your home, generally the center third section at the front of the house. Is it cluttered and dark? The universal energy, known as qi, may be stagnant or blocked, whereas it should be allowed to flow freely. Tidy your hallway and assess whether you need to install a skylight or a bright attractive lamp or lantern. A bowl of bright fresh Summer flowers will also help the energy to start moving. If you can see your back door from your front door, the qi is possibly racing through your home, not being given the opportunity to circulate its beneficial energy through your house. You might have the feeling that opportunities just race by you. Try slowing down the qi by placing wind chimes or even pot plants between the front and back doors.

Honoring the sun
— exercising your body and soul

The sequence of yogic postures or asanas called "Salute to the Sun" balances and harmonizes the body and the soul. The exercise is designed to pay homage to the life force itself by being a meditation and a physical movement all in one. The twelve postures should ideally be performed in the morning.

1. Stand straight with your legs and knees together and your hands in prayer position.

2. Inhale and stretch back your arms over your head as far as is comfortable.

3. Exhale and bend over and touch your toes. If you cannot reach your toes, try holding onto your shins.

4. Inhale and bend your knees and place your hands on either side of your feet, stretching the right foot back and placing your right knee on the floor. Tilt your head back.

5. Retain your breath and stretch back your left foot and move your hips up into the "mountain" pose. Try to keep your heels on the floor.

6. Exhale as you lower your knees, chest and forehead to the floor. Your hips should still be raised slightly higher than the rest of your body.

7. Inhale and lower your hips as you raise your upper body in the "cobra" position.

8. Exhale and raise your hips back into the mountain position.

9. Inhale and, leaving your hands where they are on the floor, bring your left foot forward, tucking the knee into your chest and keeping the right knee on the floor.

10. Exhale and straighten your left foot and bring your right foot forward, bending at the hips and keeping your hands on the floor or holding onto your shins.

11. Inhale and straighten your body, allowing your arms to sweep over your head while arching your spine back.

12. Exhale and return to standing with your feet together and your hands in prayer pose.

Repeat the exercise, but this time change sides. Begin with about one to three rounds on both sides and build up to 10 or more rounds. If the exercise is performed at the same time each day, people of the vata type will find that they become more regular in their energy level while people of the pitta type will feel calmer. Kapha people will feel particularly energized (see pages 72, 73 and 74 for identifying which body type you are). By controlling your inhalations and exhalations, this exercise becomes a meditation for the soul.

1

2

3

4

5

6

7

8

9

10

11

12

Caution

Check with your health practitioner about commencing this exercise if you
have a history of high blood pressure or heart-related problems.

Bringing new energies into your house using feng shui

Summer is a social time. It is the height of yang (or male, extrovert) energy in the year. While the home is often tidied to look attractive to guests, it is also possible to make the home attractive to other energies, such as love and wealth. Feng shui, the ancient Chinese art of design and placement based on the understanding of the flow of the universal energy (qi), has a number of tips on how to attract such positive energies into your home.

Feng shui beliefs revolve around the principles of balance and harmony, advocating that energy circulates well in a regularly shaped house. If your house is irregularly shaped, say it is "L" shaped, square off the shape and see whether there is an empty space near the back of the house on either the right- or left-hand side. If there is, you may be having trouble attracting good energy around wealth or your relationships. Using the Bagua, as you are standing at your front door, the relationship corner is near the back of the house on the right-hand side while the wealth corner is near the back of the house on the left-hand side.

It is important to make the external shape of your house rectangular or square. This can be achieved by placing an object, such as a pot plant or a garden lamp post, outside at a point where the corner of your house would be if it were regularly shaped. If your relationship corner is missing, planting a fruit blossom tree at a point that represents that missing corner will help improve your relationship and will smooth your

Increasing your wealth

To increase your wealth, place under a pot plant in your home three gold-colored coins that have been wrapped in red paper.

friendships. You may similarly square off the wealth sector with an external feature like a birdbath.

Wealth is particularly linked with yin energy and the element of water. It follows that all areas in your home dealing with water, such as sinks, bath and laundry tubs, and toilets, must be in good working order and are not blocked in any way. To ensure that you do not lose your wealth, it is important to do the following things:

- fix leaky taps immediately
- always flush your toilet with the lid down
- cover all floor drain holes
- keep the laundry and bathroom doors closed at all times.

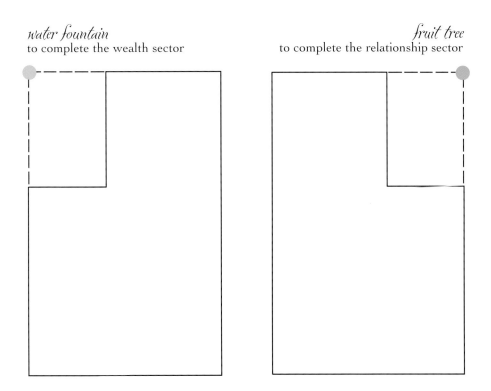

water fountain
to complete the wealth sector

fruit tree
to complete the relationship sector

Making herbal amulets of protection

An amulet is a protective device which can be worn on the body. It can take the form of a symbol, such as a cross or a pentacle, or a pouch that contains herbs, stones or other substances. The contents of a protection amulet may include substances that treat an illness you wish to avoid.

Dried herbs have traditionally been incorporated as part of an amulet. To make your own amulet, first think of a specific event, illness or form of negativity from which you seek protection. This will help you choose your particular herb. You will have been able to harvest quite a number of herbs in Summer, each having its own meaning.

Herbs need to be cut when the day is dry and hung on string in a dry room. Traditionally your herbs should be cut at full moon if you wish to bring health, and between waning and new moon if you wish to get rid of disease. If you are going to use the herbs to assure the beginning of a new project, it is recommended you cut the herbs at new moon.

To contain the herbs, a small bag can be crafted from a circle of leather or silk with a leather thong or silk ribbon threaded through the circumference. Knot the ends of the thong and pull the circle into a small bag within which you can insert a muslin bag with the appropriate herb or mix of herbs and a little blessing, perhaps written on a piece of parchment.

Certain herbs are particularly effective when made up as amulets. Saint John's wort, which is gathered at Summer solstice, is an excellent herb for protection. When finished making your amulet, sprinkle some chamomile into the amulet as the herb is renowned for its promise of success.

Other protective herbs
Fennel • Garlic • Ginger • Hyssop • Valerian

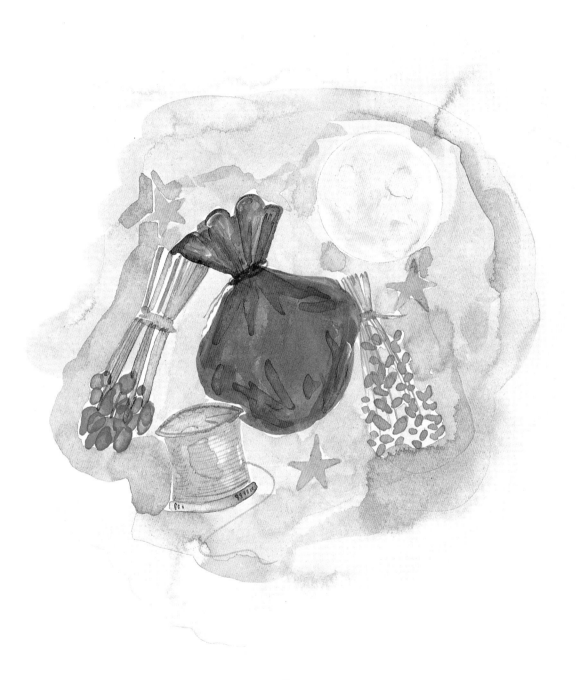

AUTUMN
The Season of Balance
The final harvest

"Season of mists and mellow fruitfulness."
John Keats (1795 – 1821), *To Autumn*

In Autumn we are gathering in the last harvest, stocking up on extra firewood, making conserves and jams to last us through Winter and changing our diets to heavier foods. Echoing the season, this is the time when we are consolidating our energies, fine-tuning what we have achieved since Spring and starting to build up our reserves for Winter. As the weather gets colder and colder, the more reliant we are on the warmth and protection of our homes. Making your home a haven by correcting the flow of energy in your house can help consolidate your energy (see pages 54 and 55 for a table of solutions to common problems). As the days become shorter, create more light for your home by making scented candles (see pages 56 and 57).

Autumn is also the time to regulate the energies within your body. This can be achieved through balancing the different energies of the food you eat (see pages 46 and 47) and by using gentle balancing exercises (see pages

52 and 53). As the final harvest is brought in, the energy of the season shifts from active to contemplative. This might be a time to delve deeper and look at neglected areas, such as how you breathe. Learning to breathe properly can help alleviate stress and manage the onset of asthma and other respiratory problems (see pages 48 and 49). Finding your equilibrium will also strengthen you so that you can address any stagnant energy in your home and workplace which might be affecting your career (see pages 50 and 51).

Celebrating the Autumn equinox

The Autumn equinox, the signal for the start of Autumn, has a dual role. It is the time of the primary harvest; on the other hand, it is also the time for determining what we will need for Winter. The beginning of Autumn is a time of balance between light and dark, of yin and yang energies and between life and death. Traditionally, this was the time of the second harvest, the grape harvest. Celebrations during this time focused on giving thanks to the spirit of the land and preparations were made for the quiet time of Winter ahead.

In the Northern Hemisphere, six weeks after the Autumn equinox, the Halloween festival occurs at the height of Autumn's powers. This is the time of the third and final harvest — the fruit and nut harvest. Traditionally, as Halloween was the time of the apple harvest, its festivities included bobbing for apples and being given candy apples as a trick-or-treat gift. Halloween is a time when you may wish to focus your mind on what study and resolutions you may need to devote yourself to throughout the contemplative Winter months. It is a time to ask for guidance for using Winter wisely so that your energy reserves build to a peak that will power you through to the Summer Solstice. You may also seek guidance for the development of your inner self. If you are in the Southern Hemisphere, celebrate this festival on 1 May.

Your Autumn diet and garden

Autumn is the time for helping your digestive system achieve a balance between yin and yang energies. In the body, yin and yang energies correspond with acid and alkaline states respectively. A number of health regimes that focus on the way we eat, such as food combining, can help our bodies achieve balance between acid and alkaline states.

Fruit and vegetables are easier to digest than proteins, such as steak or cheese, and starches, such as bread. Many fruit and vegetables are categorized as alkaline-forming while most proteins are acid-forming and take longer to digest. There are only a few basic rules that should be observed to follow a food-combining diet, for example:

- avoid combining starch and protein
- eat fruit by itself or before a meal.

It is advised that the three meals of the day should follow the following pattern:

- one alkaline-forming meal (using only fruit or vegetables — perhaps a vegetable stir fry for dinner or a couple of fruits for breakfast);
- one protein meal (which is a balance between acid-forming protein and alkaline-forming vegetables — imagine a lamb roast with honeyed carrots, buttered broccoli and cauliflower); and
- one starch meal (which is a balance between acid-forming starch and alkaline-forming vegetables — for example, spaghetti with a vegetarian sauce of tomato, basil and garlic).

Advice

When increasing the amount of fresh fruit and vegetables in your diet, be careful to wash them thoroughly and, if the produce is not organic, discard the peel. Try as much as possible to obtain organic fruit and vegetables — or better still, grow them yourself.

Autumn fruits and vegetables

Fruit	Vegetables
Apples	Broccoli
Avocados	Brussels sprouts
Figs (early Autumn)	Butternut pumpkin
Grapes	Button squash (early Autumn)
Limes	Cabbage (mid Autumn)
Mandarins (late Autumn)	Capsicums (early Autumn)
Melons	Cauliflower (mid Autumn)
Peaches (early Autumn)	Celery
Pears (Packham)	Choko
Plums	Corn (early Autumn)
Cantaloupes (rockmelons) (early Autumn)	Aubergines (Eggplants)
Watermelon (early Autumn)	Leeks (mid Autumn)
	Parsnips (mid Autumn)
	Swedes (mid Autumn)
	Tomatoes (early Autumn)
	Zucchini

Your Autumn gardening tasks

At the beginning of Autumn you may wish to sow red beet (beetroot), cauliflower, lettuce and radishes, and plant the shallots. By mid Autumn, many of the vegetables must be harvested, particularly the pumpkins and potatoes, and cuttings of lavender, mint, rosemary and sage should be taken. Mid Autumn is a good time to sow Spring and Winter flowering bulbs, such as tulips and ranunculas.

Pranayama — learning to breathe

How we breathe is often neglected. Focusing on our breath is useful in alleviating stress and such respiratory problems as asthma. Often stress makes us contract our diaphragm, as if we have been hit in the stomach, and this can force us to breathe shallowly. After a period of sustained shallow breathing, we may experience a feeling of anxiety and even depression. There is a school of thought that the inability to breathe properly can even cause asthma.

In both Chinese and Ayurvedic traditional medicine, breathing exercises are advocated to correct any respiratory irregularities. The Indian form is called pranayama which means the control of breath, the control of the prana or life force. Pranayama is a series of exercises that teach breath control and specifically promote breathing predominantly through the nose, rather than the mouth.

The first step to learning a good breathing technique is to become aware of your breath. Lie down or sit comfortably. In the Iyengar form of yoga, a special bolster or a few rolled up blankets are placed under your back and neck, helping the chest expand as you consciously release the tensions in your body.

As you lie or sit quietly, visualize each major body part from your toes

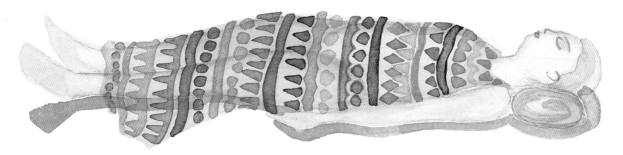

to your head relaxing, paying particular attention to relaxing your eyes into their sockets, quieting your ear drums, stilling your vocal chords and tongue. Allow your tongue to rest on the lower palate and check that your jaw muscles are unclenched.

The next step is to observe your breath. Do not attempt to change what your breath is doing at this stage, just feel the rhythm of your breathing. Is it irregular? Is it shallow? Keep your feeling of relaxation. Passively watch your breath. As you are watching your breath, you might feel tension, perhaps an old injury. Quietly observe where you feel the tension, consciously relaxing those areas again.

Try this exercise for ten minutes each day. You will feel like your inner reserves are being restored, as well as certain tensions that normally occurred when you breathed are released. In the orthodox yogic tradition, it is advised that you learn further pranayama techniques under expert tuition. If this technique interests you, there are many yoga schools that you can investigate.

Advantages of a good breathing technique

- *Calms the nervous system*
- *Increases our energy levels*
- *Carries oxygen into our blood stream*

Fine-tuning your workplace

"Give your best and always be kind."
Epictetus (55 AD – 135 AD)

Autumn is the time of harvest. All the effort you have made in changing your career path should start paying off in this season, particularly at its beginning. For some, an opportunity already would have presented itself that will allow you to follow your life's work. For others, the benefits that you are harvesting may be much more subtle. Make an audit of all that you have done so far and look at what information, images and useful people you have found to help support your change. How strong is your resolve to make the change happen?

As Autumn progresses, you will find that the energy of the season becomes passive and more introspective. This might be the time not only to assess and strengthen your resolve to make a change in your career but to also fine-tune your workplace, whether you are enjoying a new change or are still finding your feet. If you work at a desk, you might find it interesting to apply the Bagua to your workplace. You can subdivide your desk in the following segments.

To encourage good fortune in a particular area, place a vase of flowers or a picture of bright colored flowers or a package of three coins wrapped in red paper in the area.

Wealth	*Fame*	*Relationships*
Background Information	*Health*	*New projects*
Inner wisdom	*Career/ lifestyle*	*Help from people*

Chair

In many workplaces, we sit in a position with our backs to the main entry of our office. This is bad feng shui as it promotes low-grade anxiety or the apprehension that you will be disturbed in your work without warning. If you are not able to move your desk to face the door or opening in the partition, you might try imagining a shield of blue energy shielding the door from intrusion. Honor the image by lowering the shield each time you want to leave your office. You could also place a mirror on your desk to reflect the doorway.

If you want to encourage luck to enter your workplace, you might consider using some of the symbols of feng shui as good-luck amulets. You could make a flat disc of paper, wood, ceramic or metal and inscribe the symbols outlined in the table below which are appropriate for success in your career. If you have made an amulet in Summer, you might like to put the disc into the amulet bag and wear it to work, close to your heart.

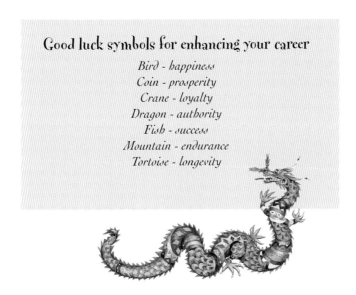

Good luck symbols for enhancing your career

Bird - happiness
Coin - prosperity
Crane - loyalty
Dragon - authority
Fish - success
Mountain - endurance
Tortoise - longevity

Finding and keeping your balance
— some gentle exercises

The beginning of Autumn is considered a time of balance in Chinese medicine traditions. It is a good time to incorporate one or two simple, gentle exercises to help you remember and maintain a sense of balance in your life for the rest of the year. Try to include at least one such exercise each day for a year and a day. This commitment will soon repay your effort as you will become aware of a sense of well-being and stability in your life.

One exercise, which is very simple yet powerful, is to visualize a cord extending from just above your head, through your spine and into the earth. While sitting or standing comfortably, imagine the central vertical axis of your body aligning with that cord. Hold this image in your mind for about five minutes. Inevitably, unbidden images of your life or trivia, such as the shopping list, will come into your head. Gently let the images go, watch them leave, and return to your initial image of the cord. You will find that after a few weeks of practice, you will be able to hold this image for longer with much less effort.

If you have been practicing this exercise standing up, you may wish to extend the exercise by including a further element. Make sure you are standing with your feet and knees together. Attempt to feel the muscles in the front of your legs pushing back against those in the back of your legs. Feel the interplay of the muscles. Once you have balanced the sensations in the front and back of your legs, try it from the sides, the right and left sides of your leg muscles pushing inward. Allow this feeling to travel up the trunk of your body.

What you should be feeling, if you haven't fallen over, is your body working to balance itself. By learning to pull your body into its center you are helping the mind to accomplish the same result so that it can collect its straying energies and concentrate them into your core. You could also imagine that you are a tree being buffeted by the forces of the four elements — air, fire, water and earth. By combining the mind's effort with the body's, you will start to feel integrated and balanced within your body and your soul.

Correcting the flow of energies
in your home

Feng shui gives us a number of simple and practical solutions for poor flows of energy through your home. According to the principles of feng shui, positive energy (sheng qi) can be encouraged along gently curving lines while negative energy (sha qi) flows in straight lines. It is important that the universal energy (qi) is encouraged to flow through your house without obstructions and at an easy pace, bringing with it good luck, prosperity and well-being. If the energy becomes obstructed or is encouraged to move in straight lines, the energy can become stagnant or destructive.

In the table opposite, you will find a number of common problems identified as blocking or dispersing qi matched with a feng shui solution that will help allow the energy to move more freely around your home. Use your intuition about what solutions to adopt. Try one at a time and learn to sense whether you have correctly identified your problem.

PROBLEM	SOLUTION
House facing busy street	*Plant trees, shrubs or build a wall to screen the fast moving energy away from your house; install a weather vane or place a small mirror on the wall of the house facing the street*
Irregularly shaped land	*Plant in the corners to angle the energy away from stagnating in the corners*
Irregularly shaped house	*Plant a tree or shrub or place a lamp at a point in the garden to make the house appear to be a square or a rectangle — this will help balance the energies in the house*
L-shaped rooms	*Create two separate spaces divided by a screen or piece of furniture*
Front door often in shade	*Hang wind chimes near the door to stimulate positive energy (sheng qi)*
Front and back doors facing each other	*Hang a crystal or wind chimes inside the front door*
Window overlooking blank wall or displeasing prospect	*Place cheerful plants along the window sill or frame the window with pleasing draperies*
Stairs facing front door	*Place wind chimes or crystal between the foot of the stairs and the front door*
Dark living room	*Install a fish tank or include lively, cheerful colors in your decorating*
Bathroom in center of the house	*Install a skylight or hang mirrors*
Dark bathroom	*Include green indoor plants in bathroom decor and use bright colors*
Chair, bed, desk under a beam	*Move the furniture or hang bamboo flutes from the beam*
Chair back facing door	*Move the furniture so that you are facing the door*
Mirror or electronic equipment facing bed	*Cover mirror, computer screen or TV with a cloth*
Stove facing kitchen door	*Install a mirror behind the stove burners*

Creating scented sand candles

Traditional Autumnal duties often included the making of inventories of household items to ensure that all essential items were plentiful during Winter. If stocks of candles were becoming low, they were either bought or made during Autumn. The following project is an easy no-fuss way of making natural-looking candles that can be scented with your favorite essential oil.

You will need some wet sand in a box or container, wax, wick and a double boiler. Your double boiler can be a clean tin can that fits inside a saucepan. The idea is to put the wax in the tin can which is then placed in a saucepan of boiling water. As the wax melts, you can add a few drops of essential oil into the mix.

The size of your box of sand depends on how many candles you want to make, it can be 1–2 feet (up to 1 m) square box if you want to make several or you could even use a number of smaller produce boxes. It is important that the box is fairly sturdy and at least 6–8 inches deep. You can get sand

from a variety of sources, ranging from your local nursery to a nearby beach. Fill your box with sand and hose it with water to make sure it is thoroughly wet. Then, while the wax is melting, hollow out one to four holes in the sand, about 4–6 inches (8–15 cm) in diameter and about 2–3 inches (4–6 cm) deep. You can texture the hollows with a light sprinkling of fairly well-ground dried herbs. To make legs, stick a pencil at an angle in three or four points at the bottom of your hollow.

Once the wax has melted, get a length of wick and hold it near the center of each hollow while you pour the wax into the hollow. Once set, the candle can be lifted out of the sand. Once you have brushed off the excess sand, the candles are ready for use. Try them in your bathroom to light a romantic bath.

Aromatherapy oils

Basil — clarifies the mind
Bergamot — uplifts the nerves
Cedarwood — stabilizes emotions
Geranium — cleanses emotions
Lavender — calms emotions and nerves
Marjoram — relieves grief
Orange — aids sleep and relaxation
Peppermint — overcomes shock
Rosemary — relieves mental fatigue
Sandalwood — stimulates confidence
Ylang ylang — relieves depression

WINTER
The Season of Reflection
A time for contemplation

Without valleys, there are no mountains

In Winter, the energy in the garden has gone underground and is no longer tangibly visible (see page 61). It is the time to prune, mulch and feed the earth, nurturing it for Spring's new growth. So too must we relax and recuperate during this season, paying particular attention to the foods that will help us rest and build up our energy reserves (see page 60). It is also a time to build up our protection, in terms of both our bodies (see pages 62 and 63) and our homes (see pages 68 and 69).

As we move toward the Winter equinox, the days become shorter. In climates where the seasons are distinct, the shortage of light has been known to affect people's sense of well-being. The onset of depression during Winter ("the Winter blues") is common and is now scientifically known as Seasonal Affective Disorder (or SAD). However, there are some easy ways that can help alleviate this feeling (see pages 66 and 67).

At the darkest time of the year, a light is born that will lead us to the Spring. Traditionally, the birth of a sun deity heralded the beginning of new hope. Winter is the time of quietly studying your plans and making sure that each aspect is within a cohesive structure that allows you to succeed (see pages 64 and 65). You may even wish to focus upon what you have achieved in life by using colorful fabrics and shapes to make yourself a magical appliquéd quilt.

Celebrating the Winter solstice

The Winter solstice, or Yule, is known in the Christian calendar as Christmas, the time of the birth of Christ. The Sun is at its lowest point in the heavens. The birth of new promise and hope is celebrated at this time because from this day onward the nights will again become shorter and the days will be longer.

The Anglo-Saxon word "Yule" means "wheel" and is said to be a reference to the Wheel of the Year. Bringing a young evergreen tree into the home was one of the traditions of Yule. The tree was decorated with fruits, berries and nuts, symbolizing the continuity of the seasons' cycle and the cycle of life itself. Another tradition linked with trees is the burning of the Yule log. This symbolizes the return of warmth and light.

Personal rituals around Yule can focus on what your new plans are going to be for the new year. You may at this time receive some insight into what path you may take in the new cycle. If you are burning the Yule log, look into the flames for a while and sometimes the smoke or the shape of the burning wood can give you images or symbols that can help you choose your truc path.

Your Winter diet and garden

Winter is the time to rest and to release the stress accumulated throughout the past year. In Chinese medicine, food is often used to heal the body. There is a particularly effective soup that can be made in Winter to help with your rest. It is a tasty combination of shiitake mushrooms (half a dozen that have been soaked in water for half an hour), a sea vegetable called kombu, two shallots, tamari sauce to taste and some udon noodles. Called dashi stock soup, it is a powerfully regenerative soup.

Shiitake mushrooms help dissolve excess animal fats and have been used for the treatment of the immune system. They are especially known for relaxing a tense and stressed body. It is best to take this soup only once every few days, rather than consecutively.

Dried seaweed is now available in supermarkets. Seaweed is of particularly high nutritional value and low in fat. It can be introduced into the diet with rice or in soups in small, almost unnoticeable, but still beneficial, quantities. It is marvelous for the thyroid gland and can help with weight-control diets. To use, just soak the seaweed in water for ten minutes to half an hour and then gently remove from the water with your fingers, throwing away the residue.

Another staple medicinal food advocated by Chinese medicine is miso soup. Made from miso paste, which is in turn made from fermented soy beans, miso soup is a wonderful dish to have before your evening meal. The taste is very pleasant, salty and savory, and it is famous for aiding digestion and having a calming effect on your stomach. It has also been known to help reduce high cholesterol levels. For Winter, use either hatcho miso or mugi miso (fermented barley), while for Summer, you can use a lighter fermented paste called shiro miso, which actually tastes quite sweet. It is important that you never put miso into boiling water as this can destroy the beneficial enzymes in the paste.

Winter Fruits and Vegetables

FRUIT	VEGETABLES
Apples	Red beet (beetroot)
Avocados	Broccoli
Mandarins	Brussels sprouts
Oranges (Navel)	Butternut pumpkin (early Winter)
Pears (Packham)	Cabbage
Plums (early Winter)	Cauliflower
Strawberries (late Winter)	Celery
	Choko
	Aubergines (Eggplants) (mid Winter)
	Green beans
	Leeks
	Parsnips
	Snow peas
	Swedes
	White turnip
	Zucchini (Courgette) (mid Winter)

Your gardening tasks in Winter

Winter is the time to plant your asparagus, garlic and shallots, and sow your cabbage, onions and peas. By mid Winter, you will need to consider what vegetable plantings you will need to do for the new year and perhaps investigate the idea of rotating crops. It is also time to tidy up your perennials by cutting back their leaves.

Garden journal

Consider starting a gardening journal in which you can keep track of the progress of your vegetable and herb gardens, noting what grew well and when various plants grew best. You could also keep a note of each season's weather patterns in your area.

Protecting your body from the Winter chills

Winter is a time to strengthen your immune system to help it counteract the colds and flu prevalent in the season. There are a number of traditional recipes, using herbs and other foods, that you can try if you begin to feel unwell.

Herbal solutions

The successful use of vitamin C for colds has been demonstrated scientifically, showing its ability to lessen the severity of the illness. Many berries and fruits contain high dosages of Vitamin C. Try rosehip tea, using a handful of carefully washed fresh rosehips with a cup of boiling hot water. You may wish to sweeten the drink with a teaspoon of honey.

Echinacea, known as a cleanser of blood, is also useful for alleviating the symptoms of a cold.

Garlic is excellent for preventing colds or nursing you through a Winter chill. There are now very effective odorless garlic capsules available or, if you want something natural for your cough, try a tablespoon of your own homemade mixture of four or five garlic cloves with half a cup of honey. You can store your mixture in the pantry cupboard in a sterilized jar. Look out for organic garlic cloves, which are stronger in flavor than the commercially grown variety.

Medicinal foods

Medicinal vegetables, such as cabbage, can be useful curatives for the Winter chills. Cabbage is reputed to have the ability to remove toxins from the body if used as a compress. The leaves can be placed between two sheets of pure cotton cloth and can be scrunched with a rolling pin so that the leaves release their juice. If your cold moves to your chest, making your lungs feel congested and sore, use the cabbage compress on your chest, either front or back, or on the back of the neck. Wrap an old, clean towel around your chest and the compress so that your clothes do not get stained by the mixture.

Mustard compresses are also used to warm the chest and help with chest colds.

White cabbage, which is plentiful during Winter, is invaluable for easing the feeling of stiffness in the joints. Use it as a base for your Winter soups, frying it in a tablespoon of oil with onion, garlic and carrots. And, of course, don't forget a bowl of hot chicken soup, which has actually been scientifically proven to help combat congested mucus.

Learning to act out your will

"Learning can be defined as the process of remembering what you are interested in."
R.S. Wurman

Winter is the time to study, either to enhance your knowledge of your current job or to assess whether your plans for a career change have been cohesively structured. There is a school of thought that once you have decided where your career is leading, you have essentially set up a path along which tendencies and circumstances in your life will also move. In Western magical traditions it is said that, by concentrating intently on what you wish to happen, you open an "astral doorway" to a new reality where what you want to bring into being will actually happen. But your intention must be strong. There is a famous saying in magic — "Do what thou wilt shall be the whole of the Law." The key to this philosophy is that you need to be very clear of your true will, attuning your goals to the often hidden purposes of your Higher Self.

Ancient Wisdom
Nothing truly stops you. Nothing truly holds you back.
For your own will is always within your control.
Epictetus (55 AD– 135 AD)

You have already decided, in Spring, what is your "will" concerning your career. Your will has been strengthened in Summer by consistently building a portfolio of images and information about your choice. In Autumn, you have cleared the energetic paths in your work place and at home to help your purpose

Short checklist for career success
·Focus your will
·Feel confident in your power to change
·Weigh the merits of the change
·Visualize your successful career

along. In Winter, you take the next step by imagining the success of your plan. For instance, imagine sitting in a new office with a nice healthy pay check in the drawer. Imagine everything about the office and visualize how you look and feel in the new environment.

If you notice that your mind starts to wander when trying to visualize the success of your project, it might be worthwhile to do a few visualization exercises. Try focusing on a photograph of a landscape, noticing all the details it contains. Once you feel confident that you know the picture well, tear the photograph in half. Put one half on the table in front of you and try to visualize the other half.

Coping with depression

As the days become darker, many people may start to feel down and some may even feel close to suicidal. The "Winter blues" has now been scientifically acknowledged as "Seasonal Affective Disorder" (or SAD) and is known to have affected close to ten million people a year.

There is a theory that SAD occurs because the shortening of daylight affects a person's personal rhythm. The rhythm between waking and sleeping is particularly disrupted when the body is required to wake up when it is still dark. This lack of light is cited as one of the major causes of SAD. Light activates the body's pineal gland to stop secreting a hormone called melatonin which helps the body sleep. If there is insufficient light the gland continues to secret melatonin, keeping the body feeling tired.

If our working life followed seasonal timing, we would avoid this problem by simply sleeping more during Winter, which, traditional Chinese medicine tells us, is the appropriate thing to do at this time of the year. However, many of us work rigid hours that cannot be seasonally adjusted and our waking time is governed by the alarm clock rather than the sun.

To ease the feeling of SADness, health practitioners have advised using light to correct the condition. Solutions include spending more time outdoors enjoying a brisk walk or doing your exercises. Other advice includes sleeping with your curtains drawn so that you see the first light of dawn. Sufferers can also obtain light therapy or phototherapy from specially trained health practitioners who expose the patient to a certain voltage of artificial light in the form of fluorescent tubes. The use of light as a

Signs of SADness
The following symptoms have been noted in people who have suffered SAD:
- *lack of energy*
- *feeling sleepy all the time*
- *troubles concentrating*
- *cravings for certain foods, particularly carbohydrates*
- *weight gain*
- *loss of libido*

therapy has been known to have a beneficial effect on balancing hormonal levels, promoting healing and helping eliminate sleeping disorders.

It would be interesting to speculate whether, at the other end of the scale, the lengthening of days during midsummer can also adversely affect a person's rhythm and be the cause of the feeling of lethargy and disruption that often occurs at Midsummer's Eve.

Aromatherapy solutions

If you are feeling only mildly depressed over Winter, try one or a combination of the following essential oils to uplift your spirits:

- *lemon*
- *orange*
- *lavender*
- *clary sage*
- *rose*
- *ylang ylang*
- *bergamot*
- *geranium*

Protection spells for your home

You can do a protection spell for your home in Winter, particularly if you have experienced any grief, relationship disturbances or other sadness during the last year.

For the protection ritual, you will need a white candle and a bowl of salted water. You may also wish to prepare some herbs to place at doorways and windows for protection. Fennel or a sprig of St. John's wort, saved from your Midsummer's Eve gathering, can be hung over the entrance doors, and a bunch of fennel may be used to splash salt water around the house and to sprinkle the water around each door and window to cleanse the space. Other herbs, such as camphor or caraway, could also be used in the water.

Place your candle and matches at your front door along with your bundles of herbs. Tie your bundles with a piece of red-colored string. Taking your bowl of salted water (with or without herbs), walk slowly around the outside of your house and splash water around its perimeter. It is important to follow the motion of the sun, walking around your house in a clockwise motion in the Northern Hemisphere or anti-clockwise in the Southern Hemisphere. Keeping the appropriate motion, enter the house and light the candle at the entrance.

Move through the house from room to room, concentrating on the candle and keeping an eye on where you are going. In each room splash some of the water at the door and at all windows. If appropriate, take your basket of herbs and place one bundle above each door and window.

If you work with needle and thread, you may consider this other spell to protect your house. Each time you finish with a bit of thread and there is some left over, put the leftover thread into a small jar with the words "protect this house from hardship and harm." Eventually the jar will fill up and can be sealed with a protective herb and stored in the highest place in the house.

To anchor these spells, you could also plant basil or dill in a window box or herb garden to keep bringing you protection and good fortune, or plant a tree such as the rowan or mountain ash to watch over your house and family.

Making a quilt block
— appliqué the landmarks of your life

The magic of quilting can be harnessed in the Winter season as you use symbols and traditional quilting patterns to show all you have achieved up to this season in your life. This project complements the project you completed in Spring, which set out your ambitions and goals. We are often so busy setting our goals, that it is surprisingly easy to forget to take stock of all the blessings we have already within our life.

You may wish to use traditional quilt blocks, such as the eight-pointed star which is the symbol for abundance or a five-pointed star for luck, or you may choose to appliqué one or more of the following symbols:

Angel — kind mentor, child
(depending on how you view your relationship)
Bear — strength
Flowers — fertility/short-term creativity
Hand — friendship
Heart — love
House — stability
Oak leaves — strength
Potted plants — fertility/creativity
Star — success
Trees — long-term creativity.

Approximate measurements for the finished size
of bed cover quilts (width x length)
Single — 5½ x 8½ inches (140 cm x 210 cm)
Double — 7 x 8½ inches (180 cm x 210 cm)
Queen — 8½ x 8½ inches (210 cm x 210 cm)
King — 9¾ x 8½ inches (245 cm x 210 cm)

For your appliqué block, choose a square piece of cotton or calico, measuring 12 inches x 12 inches (30 cm x 30 cm). If you are considering making a quilt, think about using a square, measuring 6 inches x 6 inches (15 cm x 15 cm) upon which you will only need to appliqué one symbol.

If you intend to make only the one block, use the following method. Choose your fabrics and shapes and use double-sided fusible webbing to iron and fix your shape onto your block. This technique requires no sewing or maybe just a decorative blanket stitch around the edges of each shape. The webbing can be bought at most fabric stores, and it is important to follow the instructions on the packaging. With this block, you may also wish to incorporate more three-dimensional items, such as buttons, feathers or shells and use other techniques to enhance the picture, such as decorative or machine embroidery.

Once you have finished your block, you may decide to frame it, using one of a number of square frames specially designed for handicrafts. You can even use this project to appliqué your dreams and wishes for the new year.

Checklist for your Ayurvedic body type

You are a kapha type if you are or have:	Yes	No
1. broad or heavy frame		
2. wide shoulder and hips		
3. heavy weight with weight storage in the lower parts of your body		
4. skin color tends to tan easily		
5. good, smooth skin condition		
6. medium to dark brown hair		
7. soft brown eyes		
8. large, even teeth		
9. stable eating habits, except for emotional eating		
10. no real favorites as to what weather you prefer		
11. a steady sex drive		
12. keen on vigorous exercise		
13. sleep heavily		
14. a steady, calm outlook on life		
15. an ability to commit to a person or course of action		
16. a compassionate nature		
17. feeling oriented		
18. good at management		
19. slow but thorough learner		
20. enjoy having a routine		

TOTAL _____

You are a pitta type if you are or have:

	Yes	No
1. medium frame which is proportioned		
2. medium-sized shoulders and hips		
3. average weight or weight evenly distributed		
4. fair-colored skin for your racial background, prone to freckles		
5. delicate, easily inflamed skin		
6. red, blond or light brown hair		
7. hazel, light blue or green eyes		
8. medium-sized mouth and teeth		
9. irritable if not able to eat regularly		
10. a preference for colder climates		
11. a strong sex drive		
12. prefer competitive sports		
13. sleep easily and comfortably		
14. a practical outlook		
15. a belief in fair play		
16. strongly held beliefs		
17. visually oriented		
18. methodical and efficient		
19. remember easily and are slow to forget		
20. good planner and organizer		

TOTAL _____

You are a vata type if you are or have:	Yes	No
1. Very tall or very short in height		
2. Narrow shoulders and hips		
3. lean or with fat distributed just around the midriff		
4. dark colored skin for your racial background		
5. dry skin		
6. hair prone to frizzing or dandruff		
7. gray, gray blue or almost black eyes		
8. crooked or uneven teeth		
9. variable appetite		
10. a yearning for warmer climates		
11. a variable sex drive		
12. poor muscle tone		
13. light sleeper		
14. a resistance to routine		
15. a need for constant stimulation		
16. an inability to concentrate on a subject		
17. hearing oriented		
18. a love for original thoughts		
19. quick to remember quick to forget		
20. difficulty sticking to a routine		

TOTAL _____

Count all the ticks in each section. The highest total of ticks in the "Yes" column is an indication of your dominant body type. If you have a sizable number of ticks in the "Yes" column in another section, this is your secondary body type.

Living a Seasonal Life

Living a seasonal life by adjusting to the individual energies of each season is a tradition taught by many ancient civilizations and one well worth reviving in a time when we are experiencing a great deal of change and turmoil. The consistency of the seasons can teach us the old rhythms of the earth where each stage of development is considered and measured.

One of the most important messages that this book can communicate to you is that it is okay to slow down. If we incorporate the lessons of the earth in our lives, we cannot help but live a life in which we can take time to make the observations and to gather the information we need to take control of our lives rather than reacting to the changes at a moment's notice, often to our detriment.

Please consider the rhythm of the seasons as a viable option for living a life which is true to your ideals and aspirations. Begin to trust in your intuition and learn to observe the world around you. Perhaps this book has sparked some memory of traditions that your own family used to follow. Consider starting a Seasonal Journal, incorporating family traditions and looking into ancient traditions or maybe those of your nation. Incorporate into your life the traditions and ideas mentioned in this book that appeal to you. Be realistic and take only small steps in changing how you live and use this book as a start of your new journey.

Ancient Wisdom
Conduct yourself in all matters, grand and public or small and domestic, in accordance with the laws of nature. Harmonizing your will with nature should be your utmost ideal.
Epictetus (55 AD–135 AD)

Table of Seasonal Correspondences

SPRING
Spring equinox
Other names — Vernal equinox, Easter, Ostara
Herbs/flowers/plants — Tansy, honeysuckle and bulb flowers such as daffodils
Stones — Ruby
Colors — Green, yellow
Elements — Fire
Planets — Mars
Zodiac — Aries

Height of Spring Energy
Other names — May Day, Feast of the Cross, Beltane
Herbs/flowers/plants — Frankincense, marigolds, roses
Stones — Emerald, jade
Colors — Orange
Elements — Earth
Planets — Venus
Zodiac — Taurus

SUMMER
Summer solstice
Other names — Midsummer's Eve, Litha
Herbs/flowers/plants — Chamomile, fennel, St John's wort, roses
Stones — Moonstone, quartz crystal, pearl
Colors — Green, orange
Elements — Water
Planet — Moon
Zodiac — Cancer

Height of Summer Energy
Other names — Lughnasadh, Feast day for the Virgin Mary, Lammas
Herbs/flowers/plants - Frankincense, sunflowers
Stones — Topaz
Colors — Golden yellow
Elements — Fire
Planet — Sun
Zodiac — Leo

AUTUMN
Autumn Equinox
Other names — Mabon
Herbs/flowers/plants — Myrrh, sage, marigolds, passion flowers, white roses
Stones — Emerald, jade
Colors — Purple
Elements — Air
Planet — Venus
Zodiac — Libra

Height of Autumn Energy
Other names — Halloween, All Saints Day, Samhain
Herbs/ flowers/plants — Sage, cornstalks
Stones — Ruby
Colors — Black, red
Elements — Fire
Planets — Mars
Zodiac — Scorpio

WINTER
Winter solstice
Other names — Midwinter solstice, Christmas, Yule
Herbs/flowers/plants — Chamomile, frankincense, holly, mistletoe, pine, evergreen
Stones — Onyx, jet, obsidian
Colors — Red, Orange
Elements — Earth
Planets — Saturn
Zodiac — Capricorn

Height of Winter Energy
Other names — Candlemas, Feast of St. Brigid, Groundhog day, Imbolc
Herbs/flowers/plants — Lavender
Stones — Turquoise
Colors — White
Elements — Water
Planets — Uranus
Zodiac — Aquarius

Glossary

Amulet — protective device worn around the neck or hung from the door or window of a sacred space or home.

Ankh — an Egyptian hieroglyphic amulet design, symbolizing immortality.

Asana — a yoga posture.

Ayurveda — a traditional system of medicine which originated in India over 5,000 years ago.

Bagua — a grid system representing eight aspects of life identified in the *I Ching* and used to apply to feng shui.

Feng shui — a traditional system of balance, placement and design which originated in China.

Kapha — in Ayurvedic medicine, kapha is one of the Three Doshas and represents potential energy. Kapha is also a body type or prakruti, identified as broad, heavy people.

Pentacle — a five-pointed star, symbolizing the four elements (earth, air, fire and water) and the spirit. The symbol may be worn in an upright position as a protection.

Pitta — In Ayurvedic medicine, pitta is one of the Three Doshas and represents balancing energy. Pitta is also a body type or prakruti, identified as people of medium size and medium weight.

Prakruti — in Ayurvedic medicine, prakruti is the body type, either vata, pitta, kapha or a combination of types.

Prana — universal energy in Ayurvedic medicine.

Pranayama — the yogic science of proper breath control.

Qi — the Chinese word for universal energy.

Seasonal Affective Disorder (SAD) — the disruption to a person's psyche because of the diminishing of light in Winter.

Sha qi — Chinese word for negative energy.

Sheng qi — Chinese word for positive energy.

Surya Namaskara — Salute to the Sun, a yogic series of twelve postures that stimulates the mind, body and spirit.

Vata — in Ayurvedic medicine, vata is one of the Three Doshas and represents irregular energy. Vata is also a body type or prakruti, identified as active lean people.

Yang — male energy in traditional Chinese medicine, corresponding with the energy of Spring and Summer.

Yin — female energy in traditional Chinese medicine, corresponding with the energy of Autumn and Winter.

DISCLAIMER

This book is intended to give general information only and is not a substitute for professional and medical advice. Consult your health care provider before adopting any of the treatments contained in this book. The publisher, author and distributor expressly disclaim all liability to any person arising directly or indirectly from the use of, or for any errors or omissions in, the information in this book. The adoption and application of the information in this book is at the reader's discretion and is their sole responsibility.

Published by Lansdowne Publishing Pty Ltd
Sydney NSW 2000, Australia

© Copyright 1998 Lansdowne Publishing Pty Ltd

First published in 1999

Publisher: Deborah Nixon
Production Manager: Sally Stokes
Designer: Sylvie Abecassis
Editor: Cynthia Blanche
Cover illustration: Penny Lovelock
Illustrator: Joanna Davies
Project Co-ordinator: Jenny Coren

National Library of Australian Cataloguing-in-Publication Data

Beattie, Antonia.
Seasonal living: a guide to living in harmony with nature and the seasons.

ISBN 186302 653 3

1. Self-actualization (Psychology). 2. Mind and body. 3. Seasons - Miscellanea.
4. Conduct of life. I. Title

155.915

Set in Cochin on QuarkXPress
Printed in Singapore by Tien Wah Press (Pte) Ltd

Quotes from Epictetus are taken from a new interpretation by Sharon Lebell of Epictetus works in *The Art of Living: The Classic Manual on Virtue, Happiness, and Effectiveness*, 1995, Harper San Francisco.